To

Mom

From

Sydnie

Date

1/25/12

Daily Inspirations of Peace

© 2008 Christian Art Gifts, RSA
      Christian Art Gifts Inc., IL, USA

Designed by Christian Art Gifts

Printed in China

ISBN 978-1-77036-038-9

10 11 12 13 14 15 16 17 18 19 – 15 14 13 12 11 10 9 8 7 6

daily inspirations

of

peace

Carolyn Larsen

christian
art gifts®

Introduction

❧

Everyone wants peace. Busy mothers of young children, career women, parents of adult children ... people from every walk of life long for peace.

Not much peace is evident in our world. There is always one group fighting another group ... sometimes to the death.

If everyone is longing for peace, why are so few finding it? Probably because most people look in the wrong places. True, centered peace comes only from God. His peace begins deep in your heart and flows outward to engulf your life and world.

Peace in Chaos

Okay, you're a female with either a family or a career ... or a family and a career. Throw in parents, hobbies, church and who knows what else. That's when life gets chaotic. In fact, life can get so crazy that you don't have a moment's peace.

Only bad things come from chaos, my friend. Chaos drives a wedge between you and the people you love, and even affects your relationship with God. There is no time for caring about friends and loved ones and no silence to hear the still, small voice of God. The chaos can even begin to make you doubt whether you have anything to offer the world.

Peace is found only by stepping back from the busyness and finding some quiet time. Slowing down lets you reconnect with those who love you. It lets you reconnect with yourself and appreciate who you are. Solitude gives you the opportunity to hear God's voice. Those experiences will bring peace, assurance that you are loved, and confidence in God's presence and that He has a perfect plan for your life.

I will lie down and sleep in peace, for You alone, O LORD, make me dwell in safety.

Psalm 4:8

"Let them come to Me for refuge; let them make peace with Me, yes, let them make peace with Me."

Isaiah 27:5

"Peace I leave with you; My peace I give you. I do not give to you as the world gives. Do not let your hearts be troubled and do not be afraid."

John 14:27

The fruit of the Spirit is love, joy, peace, patience, kindness, goodness, faithfulness, gentleness and self-control.

Galatians 5:22-23

Now may the Lord of peace Himself give you peace at all times and in every way. The Lord be with all of you.

2 Thessalonians 3:16

Be still before the LORD and wait patiently for Him; do not fret when men succeed in their ways, when they carry out their wicked schemes.

"Be still, and know that I am God; I will be exalted among the nations, I will be exalted in the earth."

Psalm 46:10

"Come to Me, all you who are weary and burdened, and I will give you rest."

Matthew 11:28

9

I do not want the peace that passeth understanding. I want the understanding which bringeth peace.

~ Helen Keller

❧

Dear Father, my life is overloaded with activities. There's no way I can experience peace in this chaos. Help me, Father, to simplify my life. Help me to say yes to the things that help me to be the person You want me to be.

Amen.

Peace That Comes from Trust

Do you see life as an adventure? Are you always on the lookout for new experiences and do you take advantage of new opportunities? Some people are real adventurers, but some are a bit more hesitant about new experiences.

If you're one of the hesitant people it may be because new things are a bit scary. You may feel that you're not in control of your life or that it's racing forward due to the newness of things. Perhaps that's unsettling.

Trust is what will give you peace in new circumstances. Trust in God. He said in His Word that He has a plan for your life and that His plan is for good things. Of course, some experiences may not "feel" good, but the ultimate goal of growing your faith stronger and your walk with God more intense, is good.

Trust God to direct your steps and strengthen your faith. Live in peace because you trust God to take care of things.

Those who know Your name will trust in You, for You, Lord, have never forsaken those who seek You.

Psalm 9:10

Blessed is the man who makes the Lord his trust, who does not look to the proud, to those who turn aside to false gods.

Psalm 40:4

When I am afraid, I will trust in You.

Psalm 56:3

Trust in the Lord with all your heart and lean not on your own understanding.

Proverbs 3:5

You will keep in perfect peace him whose mind is steadfast, because he trusts in You.

Isaiah 26:3

The LORD is good, a refuge in times of trouble. He cares for those who trust in Him.

Nahum 1:7

"Do not let your hearts be troubled. Trust in God; trust also in Me."

John 14:1

May the God of hope fill you with all joy and peace as you trust in Him, so that you may overflow with hope by the power of the Holy Spirit.

Romans 15:13

Patience with others is Love.
Patience with self is Hope.
Patience with God is Faith.

~ Adel Bestavros

Dear Father, I know that I can't fake trust. The only way to really have peace in my life is to really trust You. So today I will try to trust You with my life.

Amen.

Peace Is "Catching"

Attitudes rub off on others. In the same way that one rotten apple infects the apples around it, attitudes are passed on from person to person. This is especially true of the female of a household – you may have heard the saying, "If the momma ain't happy, ain't nobody happy." You are the one to set the mood in the home. If your life is characterized by chaos, anxiety and worry, those around you may "catch" that and model it in their own lives. However, if your life is characterized by peace and trust, you may pass that along instead.

Being around someone who is constantly anxious and worried is emotionally draining. While being with a peaceful person is like being in an oasis. A calm place where trust flows freely.

Do you bring anxiety or peace to those around you? The foundation of peace is in knowing and trusting God. Get to know Him better and better, accept His love for you and believe that His hand is guiding your life. Find peace and infect others with it!

You hear, O Lᴏʀᴅ, the desire of the afflicted; You encourage them, and You listen to their cry.

Psalm 10:17

Therefore encourage one another and build each other up, just as in fact you are doing.

1 Thessalonians 5:11

We urge you, brothers, warn those who are idle, encourage the timid, help the weak, be patient with everyone.

1 Thessalonians 5:14

Encourage one another daily, as long as it is called Today, so that none of you may be hardened by sin's deceitfulness.

Hebrews 3:13

"To love Him with all your heart, with all your understanding and with all your strength, and to love your neighbor as yourself is more important than all burnt offerings and sacrifices."

Mark 12:33

"A new command I give you: Love one another. As I have loved you, so you must love one another."

Let us consider how we may spur one another on toward love and good deeds.

Hebrews 10:24

This is how we know who the children of God are and who the children of the devil are: Anyone who does not do what is right is not a child of God; nor is anyone who does not love his brother.

1 John 3:10

*First keep the peace within yourself,
then you can also bring
peace to others.*

~ *Thomas á Kempis*

Dear Father, I want to infect others with my peace! Help me to be so peaceful that I bring peace to those around me. Father, use me to bring peace to others.

Amen.

Peace for the World

The joke about beauty pageant contestants used to be that each one would say that her biggest dream was for world peace. It was a joke because there seemed to be little that a beauty queen could do to bring about world peace, and seriously, is there ever going to be peace in this world?

But in reality, wouldn't everyone say that they want peace in this world? Sure they would. However, when you listen to the news proclaiming the unrest around the world, it seems like an impossibility. Don't let the immensity of the topic frighten you, though.

Look around at your world, your neighborhood, friends and family. Is there peace there? If not, then let peace begin with you. Make a difference in your part of the world. If each person does that, the ripple effect will spread peace farther and wider than ever before. It may not ever be that the entire world is at peace and that various religions co-exist in peace and love, but there can be peace among those you interact with. It's a beginning.

If I rise on the wings of the dawn, if I settle on the far side of the sea, even there Your hand will guide me, Your right hand will hold me fast.

Psalm 139:9-10

"I tell you the truth, if you have faith as small as a mustard seed, you can say to this mountain, 'Move from here to there' and it will move. Nothing will be impossible for you."

Matthew 17:20

Therefore, since we have been justified through faith, we have peace with God through our Lord Jesus Christ.

Romans 5:1

Take up the shield of faith, with which you can extinguish all the flaming arrows of the evil one.

Ephesians 6:16

Because of Your great compassion You did not abandon them in the desert. By day the pillar of cloud did not cease to guide them on their path, nor the pillar of fire by night to shine on the way they were to take.

Nehemiah 9:19

Guide me in Your truth and teach me, for You are God my Savior, and my hope is in You all day long.

Psalm 25:5

You are my rock and my fortress, for the sake of Your name lead and guide me.

Psalm 31:3

Your word is a lamp to my feet and a light for my path.

Psalm 119:105

The most amiable man on earth can live at peace with his neighbor only as long as the neighbor chooses.

~ *Anonymous*

❧

Dear Father, maybe the whole world will not be at peace until Jesus comes back, but my part of the world can be more peaceful if I can be filled with peace. Help me, Father, to treat others in a way that increases peace.

Amen.

Peace in My Heart

Do you have peace deep down inside your heart or have you simply learned to portray a facade of peacefulness? Two conflicting emotions cannot rule in your heart simultaneously. Say you speak peace and convince those around you that you trust God completely, but unrest and anxiety are controlling you, they will break through your calm surface in various ways.

The question is, if you do not have peace, why not? Life will always present problems and crises. Peace shows in the way you choose to handle those circumstances. Peace comes from knowing that no matter what you face in life, you will not go through it alone. God will walk beside you. If that sounds like a Sunday school answer it may be because you haven't yet experienced real peace that comes from the knowledge that God is guiding, directing, advising and most importantly, loving you through whatever comes your way. Talk to God about your anxiety. Read His Word and listen for His voice of assurance and love.

The LORD gives strength to His people; the LORD blesses His people with peace.

Psalm 29:11

Search me, O God, and know my heart; test me and know my anxious thoughts.

Psalm 139:23

For to us a child is born, to us a son is given, and the government will be on His shoulders. And He will be called Wonderful Counselor, Mighty God, Everlasting Father, Prince of Peace.

Isaiah 9:6

Do not be anxious about anything, but in everything, by prayer and petition, with thanksgiving, present your requests to God.

Philippians 4:6

The peace of God, which transcends all understanding, will guard your hearts and your minds in Christ Jesus.

Philippians 4:7

For God was pleased to have all His fullness dwell in Him, and through Him to reconcile to Himself all things, whether things on earth or things in heaven, by making peace through His blood, shed on the cross.

Colossians 1:19-20

Let the peace of Christ rule in your hearts, since as members of one body you were called to peace. And be thankful.

Colossians 3:15

Flee the evil desires of youth, and pursue righteousness, faith, love and peace, along with those who call on the Lord out of a pure heart.

2 Timothy 2:22

Though our feelings come and go,
God's love for us does not.

~ C. S. Lewis

❧

Dear Father, peace in my heart is real peace.
Without peace deep in my heart, all other
kinds of peace will be short-lived. Help me to
get foundational peace in my heart, Lord, so
that it can spread to all other areas of my life.
Amen.

Peace When You Are Afraid

When you feel afraid it's hard to think about anything except what is making you afraid. Thoughts of what has already happened and what might still happen consume your waking mind as well as your dreams. It's hard to find peace when your heart is draped in a cloak of fear. Fear keeps your mind self-focused. You can only think of how circumstances affect you. It becomes difficult to see outside yourself and God seems to slip further and further away.

So, how can you find peace in the midst of fear? Peace only comes from believing that God is present and active in your life – believing with your heart not just with your mind. That happens by spending time in His Word, getting to know what God says about peace and trust. Then it's important to meditate in silence. Keep your mind open to what God wants to say to you. Look at your life and notice God's presence and His work in your life. It's there, you just have to pay attention. Becoming newly aware that God is working in your life will open the door to peace when you are afraid.

Even though I walk through the valley of the shadow of death, I will fear no evil, for You are with me; Your rod and Your staff, they comfort me.

Psalm 23:4

May integrity and uprightness protect me, because my hope is in You.

Psalm 25:21

The Lord is my light and my salvation – whom shall I fear? The Lord is the stronghold of my life – of whom shall I be afraid?

Psalm 27:1

Those who hope in the Lord will renew their strength. They will soar on wings like eagles; they will run and not grow weary, they will walk and not be faint.

Isaiah 40:31

"I am the Lord, your God, who takes hold of your right hand and says to you, Do not fear; I will help you."

Isaiah 41:13

The LORD your God is with you, He is mighty to save. He will take great delight in you, He will quiet you with His love, He will rejoice over you with singing.

Zephaniah 3:17

Those who are led by the Spirit of God are sons of God. For you did not receive a spirit that makes you a slave again to fear, but you received the Spirit of sonship. And by Him we cry, "Abba, Father." The Spirit Himself testifies with our spirit that we are God's children.

Romans 8:14-16

There is no fear in love. But perfect love drives out fear, because fear has to do with punishment. The one who fears is not made perfect in love.

1 John 4:18

Peace is not the absence of conflict,
but the ability to cope with it.

~*Anonymous*

❧

Dear Father, I try to have peace when I'm afraid, but I get so anxious and then I start worrying. Father, I know I need to trust You to take care of me. You love me and have promised to take care of me. Please help me to trust that truth.

Amen.

The Joy of Peace

What does "peace" mean to you? Does your mind conjure up images of a person who is quiet, calm, rested and very spiritual? Well, there is no question that the benefits of living a peaceful life are numerous. Peace is possible because you have a deep confidence and trust in God.

One of the benefits of this kind of trust is that God is in His rightful place as the controller of your life. That takes the pressure off you to orchestrate life events. You can rest in the fact that God is taking care of things. A further benefit is the absence of anxiety and fear in your life. Peace is ... peaceful. What joy that brings!

If you have ever lived without peace and then made the choice to trust God completely so that you can live in peace, you know the difference. You will never want to go back to the unrest you once experienced.

Is it possible to live in peace one hundred percent of the time? Possible, but difficult. Rather celebrate the process and enjoy all moments of peace with joyful gratitude to God.

Let all who take refuge in You be glad; let them ever sing for joy. Spread Your protection over them, that those who love Your name may rejoice in You.

Psalm 5:11

The precepts of the LORD are right, giving joy to the heart. The commands of the LORD are radiant, giving light to the eyes.

Psalm 19:8

The LORD is my strength and my shield; my heart trusts in Him, and I am helped. My heart leaps for joy and I will give thanks to Him in song.

Psalm 28:7

When anxiety was great within me, Your consolation brought joy to my soul.

Psalm 94:19

The LORD has done great things for us, and we are filled with joy.

Psalm 126:3

You have made known to me the paths of life; You will fill me with joy in Your presence.

Acts 2:28

Come near to God and He will come near to you. Wash your hands, you sinners, and purify your hearts, you double-minded. Grieve, mourn and wail. Humble yourselves before the Lord, and He will lift you up.

James 4:8-10

Though you have not seen Him, you love Him; and even though you do not see Him now, you believe in Him and are filled with an inexpressible and glorious joy.

1 Peter 1:8

*Joy is the flag you fly when
the Prince of Peace is in residence
within your heart.*

~ Wilfred Peterson

❧

*Dear Father, thank You for the joy of peace.
I'm so thankful to You for loving me and
guiding and directing my life. That gives me
peace and that peace brings joy.*

Amen.

Being a Peacemaker

"If you can keep your head when all about you are losing theirs ..." then you can be a peacemaker. When people around you argue and fight, and you can manage to stay calm, you are able to bring some level of accountability to the situation. What kind of accountability? Accountability to God who instructed that those who are created in His image – mankind – should live together in love for one another. He even stated that loving one another is the second greatest commandment after loving Him.

So, being a peacemaker who encourages people to love each other is being obedient to God and helps others to be obedient to Him too.

If you can be a peacemaker who is also a peaceful person, your attitude of peace will spread to those around you. The irritations and annoyances others experience will be less likely to cause problems because the peace you live in will diffuse the situation. That's good motivation for being peaceful as well as a peacemaker.

"Love your enemies and pray for those who persecute you."

Matthew 5:44

Do not repay anyone evil for evil. Be careful to do what is right in the eyes of everybody. If it is possible, as far as it depends on you, live at peace with everyone.

Romans 12:17-18

Love is patient, love is kind. It does not envy, it does not boast, it is not proud.

I Corinthians 13:4

Aim for perfection, listen to my appeal, be of one mind, live in peace. And the God of love and peace will be with you.

2 Corinthians 13:11

But the fruit of the Spirit is love, joy, peace, patience, kindness, goodness, faithfulness, gentleness and self-control.

Galatians 5:22-23

Make every effort to keep the unity of the Spirit through the bond of peace.

Ephesians 4:3

Be kind and compassionate to one another, forgiving each other, just as in Christ God forgave you.

Ephesians 4:32

The wisdom that comes from heaven is first of all pure; then peace-loving, considerate, submissive, full of mercy and good fruit, impartial and sincere. Peacemakers who sow in peace raise a harvest of righteousness.

James 3:17-18

*Those who are at war with others are
not at peace with themselves.*
~ William Hazlett

Dear Father, sometimes I don't want to be
a peacemaker. But I know that being one is
a Christlike way to live. Help me, Father, to
remember that everything isn't about me.
Help me to think of others and to find ways
to bring peace to all.

Amen.

Peace in the Daily Grind

Sometimes life blind-sides you when you least expect it; out of the blue your boss fires you or your spouse announces that he doesn't want to be married anymore. Maybe it happens when a child turns her back on the values she was raised with or when a loved one is suddenly killed.

These are examples of the big things that life throws at you. On a more daily basis there are things like deadlines, bosses to please, misunderstandings with family members, rebellious kids ... well, this list could go on and on, couldn't it?

Oddly enough, it is often easier to find peace in the midst of those big events than it is in the daily ins and outs of life. In the big events, there is no choice but to trust God because circumstances are out of your hands. In the more daily things, some people tend to want to handle things themselves.

If you can experience peace in the daily ins and outs of life you understand the concept of daily dependence on God. That's where peace is found.

Let us not become weary in doing good, for at the proper time we will reap a harvest if we do not give up.

Galatians 6:9

We know that in all things God works for the good of those who love Him, who have been called according to His purpose.

Romans 8:28

Cast your cares on the LORD and He will sustain you; He will never let the righteous fall.

Psalm 55:22

The LORD upholds all those who fall and lifts up all who are bowed down.

Psalm 145:14

A man of knowledge uses words with restraint, and a man of understanding is even-tempered.

Proverbs 17:27

Yet this I call to mind and therefore I have hope: Because of the LORD's great love we are not consumed, for His compassions never fail.

Lamentations 3:21-22

"Therefore, if you are offering your gift at the altar and there remember that your brother has something against you, leave your gift there in front of the altar. First go and be reconciled to your brother; then come and offer your gift."

Matthew 5:23-24

Who is wise and understanding among you? Let him show it by his good life, by deeds done in the humility that comes from wisdom.

James 3:13

*When you find peace within yourself,
you become the kind of person who
can live at peace with others.*

~ *Peace Pilgrim*

*Dear Father, problems can be overwhelming.
But thank You for providing peace to keep me
steady and calm, day in and day out.*

Amen.

Peace When Things Don't Go the Way I Want

Whatever circumstances you face in life, you no doubt pray about them and ask God for His intervention and direction. You have an opinion of how you desire these things to turn out and you are probably asking God to take care of things in those ways.

What happens when things don't go the way you want? Are you able to find peace even when you don't get your way? You can't if you're not submissive and humble before God.

If you've been trying to tell God how to run His world; in a sense displacing Him from His position as powerful and sovereign God, then you will not experience peace when He doesn't do what you want.

Letting go of your own agenda and allowing God to do what He wants, in the time frame He chooses, is the only pathway to peace. Then, regardless of what your desires are, when God doesn't jump when you ask Him to, you'll be okay with it. You are more likely to have peace if you trust God with the bigger picture.

He is the image of the invisible God, the firstborn over all creation. For by Him all things were created: things in heaven and on earth, visible and invisible, whether thrones or powers or rulers or authorities; all things were created by Him and for Him. He is before all things, and in Him all things hold together.

Colossians 1:15-17

"Therefore, whoever humbles himself like this child is the greatest in the kingdom of heaven."

Matthew 18:4

He mocks proud mockers but gives grace to the humble.

Proverbs 3:34

"For whoever exalts himself will be humbled, and whoever humbles himself will be exalted."

Matthew 23:12

In all your ways acknowledge Him, and He will make your paths straight.

Proverbs 3:6

"For I know the plans I have for you," declares the Lord, "plans to prosper you and not to harm you, plans to give you hope and a future."

Jeremiah 29:11

"I will instruct you and teach you in the way you should go; I will counsel you and watch over you."

Psalm 32:8

Now listen, you who say, "Today or tomorrow we will go to this or that city, spend a year there, carry on business and make money." Why, you do not even know what will happen tomorrow. What is your life? You are a mist that appears for a little while and then vanishes. Instead, you ought to say, "If it is the Lord's will, we will live and do this or that."

James 4:13-15

Peace is the deliberate adjustment of my life to the will of God.

~ *Anonymous*

❧

Dear Father, sometimes it's hard to accept things that don't go the way I want them to. I know I need to trust You more so that I can adjust to Your will. Help my faith to grow stronger so my trust in You will deepen.

Amen.

Living in Peace with Others

Humanity is the most amazing creation of God ... it's the people I can't stand. That's a paraphrase of a well-known statement. Unfortunately, sometimes it's quite true. Even people you love annoy you once in a while. Others such as co-workers, grocery store clerks or bank tellers can sometimes be a royal pain in the neck. Is it really all that important to get along with them?

Yes, it is. That doesn't mean that you must always agree with them. It doesn't even mean that you must always like them. It simply means that you must live in peace with them. Co-existing in an atmosphere of respect and honor, even of love, is sometimes demonstrated by holding your tongue; praying about your attitude, but not always attempting a deeper friendship with some people.

There's nothing to be gained by arguing or criticizing or fighting. In fact, it requires a lot of energy that could be used more effectively in other places. It also gives a negative image of the characteristics of a child of God. Live in peace and enjoy it!

Better a dry crust with peace and quiet than a house full of feasting, with strife.

Proverbs 17:1

Let us therefore make every effort to do what leads to peace and to mutual edification.

Romans 14:19

Make every effort to live in peace with all men and to be holy; without holiness no one will see the Lord.

Hebrews 12:14

Peacemakers who sow in peace raise a harvest of righteousness.

James 3:18

Better a meal of vegetables where there is love than a fattened calf with hatred.

Proverbs 15:17

He who covers over an offense promotes love, but whoever repeats the matter separates close friends.

Proverbs 17:9

"To love Him with all your heart, with all your understanding and with all your strength, and to love your neighbor as yourself is more important than all burnt offerings and sacrifices."

Mark 12:33

"My command is this: Love each other as I have loved you."

John 15:12

We are not at peace with others because
we are not at peace with ourselves,
and we are not at peace with ourselves
because we are not at peace with God.

~ *Thomas Merton*

Dear Father, peace begins with You. Father, I want to be at peace with You; then with myself; then with others around me. Father, show me how to begin this process of being at peace.

Amen.

Peace Beyond Understanding

Perhaps you know someone who has gone through a major crisis in her life such as facing a terminal disease. As you have walked along with that person on her journey, have you seen a certain kind of peace in her heart that you simply cannot understand? Have you wondered how your friend can deal with deep pain, bad news and the prospect of death, and yet have peace in her heart? How can she face this without questioning God or being anxious at all? God's peace is truly a peace beyond human understanding.

It's amazing that some people are able to find a connection with God in the dark times of life. The peace they find is real and calming. It speaks of God's love and care for them and is filled with the promise of His eternal plan. It takes them to a deeper place in their relationship with God. It is peace beyond understanding; peace that comes only from God. It is peace that comes from completely trusting God and knowing that His plan for you is perfect.

It is the spirit in a man, the breath of the Almighty, that gives him understanding.

Job 32:8

The unfolding of Your words gives light; it gives understanding to the simple.

Psalm 119:130

Blessed is the man who finds wisdom, the man who gains understanding,

Proverbs 3:13

Leave your simple ways and you will live; walk in the way of understanding.

Proverbs 9:6

How much better to get wisdom than gold, to choose understanding rather than silver!

Proverbs 16:16

The peace of God, which transcends all understanding, will guard your hearts and your minds in Christ Jesus.

Philippians 4:7

My purpose is that they may be encouraged in heart and united in love, so that they may have the full riches of complete understanding, in order that they may know the mystery of God, namely, Christ.

Colossians 2:2

I pray that you may be active in sharing your faith, so that you will have a full understanding of every good thing we have in Christ.

Philemon 1:6

There is no way to peace,
peace is the way.

~ A. J. Muste

Dear Father, I don't understand how peace works. I just know that I'm grateful for Your patience with me and for the peace that I find when I trust in You.

Amen.

Peace Below the Surface

Do you feel that it is a sign of weakness to let others see your struggles? Rather than letting others see your failures and pains, you put on a smiling face and speak wonderful words of trusting in God and His plan and you go right on with your life. Your surface appearance is peace and trust, however, below the surface there may be a churning, twisting chaos of unrest, anxiety and fear.

Do you think you get away with it because you fool the people around you into thinking that you are calmness personified? The truth is that you cannot fool God. He sees the chaos below the surface. You can't fake peace with God; in fact, you can't fake anything with Him.

So the goal is to have real, honest peace deep in your heart. The only way to have this is to trust God in both the details and the detours of life. Peace that goes deep below the surface is real peace that will carry you through life.

Those who know Your name will trust in You, for You, LORD, have never forsaken those who seek You.

Psalm 9:10

When I am afraid, I will trust in You.

Psalm 56:3

Let the morning bring me word of Your unfailing love, for I have put my trust in You. Show me the way I should go, for to You I lift up my soul.

Psalm 143:8

Surely God is my salvation; I will trust and not be afraid. The LORD, the LORD, is my strength and my song; He has become my salvation.

Isaiah 12:2

Trust in the LORD forever, for the LORD, the LORD, is the Rock eternal.

Isaiah 26:4

"Do not let your hearts be troubled. Trust in God; trust also in Me."

John 14:1

Now faith is being sure of what we hope for and certain of what we do not see.

Hebrews 11:1

Therefore, prepare your minds for action; be self-controlled; set your hope fully on the grace to be given you when Jesus Christ is revealed.

1 Peter 1:13

Faith is a bird that feels dawn breaking and sings while it is still dark.

∼ Scandinavian Saying

Dear Father, I'm learning more and more that the condition of my heart is Your main concern. Father, I ask You to increase my faith so that my heart will be stronger and healthier. Then my peace will be deep.

Amen.

Peace When a Child Rebels

Someone has said that becoming a parent is like wearing your heart on the outside of your body. This is so true. As a parent, you invest everything into teaching and caring for the life with which God has entrusted you. As you watch your little one grow and become a definite personality, you have hopes and dreams for his or her future. Usually those dreams are for more success and happiness than you have had.

Sometimes when children reach the teenage years, they rebel and turn their backs on the values and standards you've taught them. Sometimes they even reject God. That's when your out-of-body-heart breaks in two. It's difficult to find any kind of peace when your heart is breaking over a rebellious child. What can you do? Pray. Pray. Pray. Love. Love. Love.

Pray for that child and love him or her more than ever. Remember that God is in control and He sees the bigger picture. As hard as it is to let go, trust God to love your child even more than you do. Trust Him with the outcome. Give it to Him and be at peace.

Train a child in the way he should go, and when he is old he will not turn from it.

Proverbs 22:6

The rod of correction imparts wisdom, but a child left to himself disgraces his mother.

Proverbs 29:15

Discipline your son, and he will give you peace; he will bring delight to your soul.

Proverbs 29:17

May the God of hope fill you with all joy and peace as you trust in Him, so that you may overflow with hope by the power of the Holy Spirit.

Romans 15:13

Make every effort to keep the unity of the Spirit through the bond of peace.

Ephesians 4:3

Fathers, do not exasperate your children; instead, bring them up in the training and instruction of the Lord.

Ephesians 6:4

No discipline seems pleasant at the time, but painful. Later on, however, it produces a harvest of righteousness and peace for those who have been trained by it.

Hebrews 12:11

Everyone who believes that Jesus is the Christ is born of God, and everyone who loves the Father loves His child as well.

1 John 5:1

Every child born into the world
is a new thought of God,
an ever fresh and radiant possibility.
~ *Kate Douglas Wiggin*

Dear Father, help me to remember that You love my children even more than I do. You have a plan for them and You are watching over them. I can be at peace because You are in charge.

Amen.

Choosing Peace

Stop and think about the many choices you have to make in any given day. Some are no-brainers such as choosing to breathe or choosing to swallow. When you stop and think about it, there are hundreds of such choices in each day that you don't have to think about at all.

Other choices require a bit more thought – what you eat for lunch, for example. Still other choices are major life choices of careers or spouses. Did you know that having peace in your life is also a choice? As the ups and downs of life come at you faster and faster, you can either choose fear or you can choose to allow God to lead and direct your life.

Sincerely trusting in God brings peace to your life. However, it's a deliberate choice to trust God when everything in the world is pulling you in the opposite direction. Therefore, the choice for peace is a day-by-day decision, in fact, sometimes it is a moment-by-moment choice. Maybe that sounds like work, but the reward is peace – it's worth it!

Choose for yourselves this day whom you will serve, whether the gods your forefathers served beyond the River, or the gods of the Amorites, in whose land you are living. But as for me and my household, we will serve the Lord.

Joshua 24:15

How much better to get wisdom than gold, to choose understanding rather than silver!

Proverbs 16:16

I trust in Your unfailing love; my heart rejoices in Your salvation.

Psalm 13:5

I trust in You, O Lord; I say, "You are my God."

Psalm 31:14

Trust in Him at all times, O people; pour out your hearts to Him, for God is our refuge. Selah.

Psalm 62:8

Surely God is my salvation; I will trust and not be afraid. The LORD, the LORD, is my strength and my song; He has become my salvation.

Isaiah 12:2

"Put your trust in the light while you have it, so that you may become sons of light."

John 12:36

"You did not choose Me, but I chose you and appointed you to go and bear fruit – fruit that will last. Then the Father will give you whatever you ask in My name."

John 15:16

Each one has to find his peace from within. And peace to be real must be unaffected by outside circumstances.

～ Gandhi

Dear Father, I get it – it's my choice! I can choose to honor and obey You each day. I can choose to learn to trust You and then choose to accept the peace that it brings. I choose You. I choose peace.

Amen.

Peace That Comes from Confession

People don't talk about sin much; at least not about their own sin. We have learned ways to gloss over sin or justify it. It just isn't socially and spiritually acceptable to admit that we sin all the time. Instead of offering support and encouragement to fellow believers who admit to a particular struggle, some people will take a step away from them and talk about them to others (of course, that's not gossip because that would be a sin!).

Refusing to admit sin doesn't mean there is no sin. Humanity is fallen so sin is present, even in the best of people. Getting honest about sin with yourself opens the door to peace. There is relief that comes when you can finally say, "I messed up big time. I have sinned." Next comes confession and repentance. Repentance is being truly sorry for your sin, refusing to brush it off as though it were nothing. Let your heart be broken by your disobedience to God. Through this process your relationship with God is re-established and strengthened – and peace will come.

Now make confession to the Lord, the God of your fathers, and do His will.

Ezra 10:11

Then I acknowledged my sin to You and did not cover up my iniquity. I said, "I will confess my transgressions to the Lord" – and You forgave the guilt of my sin.

Psalm 32:5

"Forgive us our debts, as we also have forgiven our debtors."

Matthew 6:12

Repent, then, and turn to God, so that your sins may be wiped out, that times of refreshing may come from the Lord.

Acts 3:19

If we confess our sins, He is faithful and just and will forgive us our sins and purify us from all un-righteousness.

1 John 1:9

There is no fear in love. But perfect love drives out fear, because fear has to do with punishment. The one who fears is not made perfect in love.

1 John 4:18

This is love for God: to obey His commands. And His commands are not burdensome.

1 John 5:3

And this is love: that we walk in obedience to His commands. As you have heard from the beginning, His command is that you walk in love.

2 John 1:6

You cannot play with sin and overcome it at the same time.

~ J. C. Macaulay

Dear Father, open my eyes to the sin in my life. Help me to be truly sorry. Father, show me how confessing my sin will make room for peace in my heart.

Amen.

Peace When a Marriage Falls Apart

It's hard to think about peace when your world is falling apart. When someone you love (and who once loved you) decides to walk away, it hurts. Your life is tossed upside-down and nothing makes sense anymore. A marriage falling apart can have a domino effect on other relationships, financial insecurity, relocation, confused children, and damaged self-esteem. There is nothing easy about divorce.

Where do you find peace in a divorce? Maybe you think that saying it's even possible to have peace is a "Sunday school answer" to a painful situation.

Well, there's no denying the fact that peace does not come easily, but as you work through things, remember that God is with you. He hasn't left you to go through this alone. Your pain is real and He knows that. If you lean on Him and trust Him, God will grow your faith and teach you more about leaning on Him. As you rebuild your life, He will strengthen and teach you until one day you will suddenly realize that you have found peace.

The LORD is my strength and my song; He has become my salvation. He is my God, and I will praise Him, my father's God, and I will exalt Him.

Exodus 15:2

Look to the LORD and His strength; seek His face always.

1 Chronicles 16:11

Listen to my cry for help, my King and my God, for to You I pray.

Psalm 5:2

Even though I walk through the valley of the shadow of death, I will fear no evil, for You are with me; Your rod and Your staff, they comfort me.

Psalm 23:4

We wait in hope for the LORD; He is our help and our shield.

Psalm 33:20

For great is Your love, reaching to the heavens;
Your faithfulness reaches to the skies.

Psalm 57:10

Trust in the LORD with all your heart and lean not
on your own understanding.

Proverbs 3:5

We know that in all things God works for the good
of those who love Him, who have been called according to His purpose.

Romans 8:28

Never give up, for that is just the place and time that the tide will turn.

~ Harriet Beecher Stowe

ༀ

Dear Father, it hurts so much. I feel like part of me is gone. I feel like I've failed. Father, thank You for being with me. Thank You that I'm not alone and that in Your eyes, I have not failed. Help me to get through this.

Amen.

The Source of Peace

Everyone wants peace. We want personal peace even more than world peace. It's interesting to look around at the various ways people attempt to find peace. Some people look for it in dedication to their careers, thinking that the more successful they are, the more peace they will find.

Others seek peace in alcohol and drugs, perhaps burying their pain in the numbness these things offer. Still others look for peace in accumulating more "stuff" such as bigger houses, more money and fancier cars. Yet none of these efforts will bring true peace to your heart.

True peace comes only from the author of peace ... God Himself. It is found by living a life of submission to God, seeking to obey Him and know Him better.

Allowing God His rightful place as controller of all things takes the pressure off you to work for peace by any of the means mentioned earlier. Lasting peace comes from God ... only from God.

Seek the Lord your God, you will find Him if you look for Him with all your heart and with all your soul.

Deuteronomy 4:9

You, O Lord, keep my lamp burning; my God turns my darkness into light.

Psalm 18:28

It is God who arms me with strength and makes my way perfect.

Psalm 18:32

The Lord your God is with you, He is mighty to save. He will take great delight in you, He will quiet you with His love, He will rejoice over you with singing.

Zephaniah 3:17

"If that is how God clothes the grass of the field, which is here today and tomorrow is thrown into the fire, will He not much more clothe you, O you of little faith?"

Matthew 6:30

"With God all things are possible."

Matthew 19:26

We have not received the spirit of the world but the Spirit who is from God, that we may understand what God has freely given us.

I Corinthians 2:12

Submit yourselves, then, to God. Resist the devil, and he will flee from you.

James 4:7

"Peace I leave with you; My peace I give you. I do not give to you as the world gives. Do not let your hearts be troubled and do not be afraid."

John 14:27

All things that speak of heaven
speak of peace.
~ *Philip James Bailey*

❧

Dear Father, I waste so much time trying to find peace in "stuff", when I know that the only place to find peace is in You. I'm sorry for wasting so much time. Help me to seek peace in You alone.

Amen.

Peace in My Family

Family – those you know the best are the ones with whom you are most honest. They know the real you and you know their true selves. All the facades that are put on for friends or co-workers are dropped. The bumps of quirky personalities come through loud and strong. Habits become irritants that annoy and anger other family members. That means family life is anything but peaceful. The sad thing is that we work very hard on establishing and maintaining peace with friends and co-workers, but do not place such a big emphasis on family peace.

Is it that hard to have a peaceful relationship with your family members? Well, yes, sometimes it is hard and it does require deliberate choices to give family members the benefit of the doubt, as you might do for others. You have a choice to forgive hurts and accept the various quirks of family members' personalities. It isn't always easy, but the peace that these efforts bring to the entire family honors God and creates a safe haven for family members.

Hatred stirs up dissension, but love covers over all wrongs.

Proverbs 10:12

Jesus replied: "'Love the Lord your God with all your heart and with all your soul and with all your mind.' This is the first and greatest commandment. And the second is like it: 'Love your neighbor as yourself.' "

Matthew 22:37-39

"To love Him with all your heart, with all your understanding and with all your strength, and to love your neighbor as yourself is more important than all burnt offerings and sacrifices."

Mark 12:33

"Greater love has no one than this, that he lay down his life for his friends."

John 15:13

If I speak in the tongues of men and of angels, but have not love, I am only a resounding gong or a clanging cymbal.

I Corinthians 13:1

Love does not delight in evil but rejoices with the truth.

I Corinthians 13:6

Therefore, as we have opportunity, let us do good to all people, especially to those who belong to the family of believers.

Galatians 6:10

If a widow has children or grandchildren, these should learn first of all to put their religion into practice by caring for their own family and so re-paying their parents and grandparents, for this is pleasing to God.

I Timothy 5:4

A happy family
is but an earlier heaven.
~ *George Bernard Shaw*

❧

Dear Father, thank You for my family. I love them so much and I'm so thankful that we love each other and love being together. Thank You for the peace in our relationships. It comes from You.

Amen.

Peace in God's Plan

Are you a planner? A planner likes to have life planned out. She makes lists of what she hopes to accomplish in a day, week or month. A planner looks ahead and knows where she expects her career to be in five years' time. She has expectations for her marriage and her children. A well-thought-out plan gives her peace.

However, life seldom follows well-laid plans. Life takes detours that throw your plans off course. How well do you handle these spontaneous changes? What happens to your peace-o-meter when your plans go out the window?

Change is difficult but it is possible to maintain peace in your life through the maze of life's changes. That peace is possible when you trust in God. Trust in the fact that He's in control of your life. Trust in the fact that He wants good things for you and is guiding and directing you to serve Him and others in a way that reflects His love to the world. Look at the detours as opportunities not problems and rejoice in what they bring.

May He give you the desire of your heart and make all your plans succeed.

Psalm 20:4

The plans of the LORD stand firm forever, the purposes of His heart through all generations.

Psalm 33:11

Commit to the LORD whatever you do, and your plans will succeed.

Proverbs 16:3

In his heart a man plans his course, but the LORD determines his steps.

Proverbs 16:9

Many are the plans in a man's heart, but it is the LORD's purpose that prevails.

Proverbs 19:21

"For I know the plans I have for you," declares the LORD, "plans to prosper you and not to harm you, plans to give you hope and a future."

Jeremiah 29:11

You remain the same, and your years will never end.

Hebrews 1:12

Now listen, you who say, "Today or tomorrow we will go to this or that city, spend a year there, carry on business and make money." Why, you do not even know what will happen tomorrow. What is your life? You are a mist that appears for a little while and then vanishes. Instead, you ought to say, "If it is the Lord's will, we will live and do this or that."

James 4:13-15

Every evening I turn my worries over
to God. He's going to be up
all night anyway.

~*Mary C. Crowley*

❧

Dear Father, I'm so glad that You have a plan for me. I trust You with my future. Guide me step by step. I rest in You.

Amen.

Maintaining Peace

Satan doesn't want you to be peaceful. He's going to throw all kinds of things at you in the hopes of breaking apart and shattering your peace. You know what you need to do in order to have peace in your heart: Develop your relationship with God. Spend time with Him, read His Word and let it sink into your heart. Trust God and allow Him to guide your life. Now that you know the things to do, how can Satan possibly shake you? He's a sneaky thing. Little things will begin popping up in your life. Things that irritate and annoy; minor relationship problems; small financial things; stress at work; ill children. They come quickly and so subtly that you don't really think about them. But they pile up one on top of the other and before you know it your peace is gone.

Don't let Satan get a foothold in your heart. Ask God continually to keep Satan away from you. Remind yourself often of God's love for you and that He is in ultimate control. Don't let those little issues chip away at the peace in your heart. Don't let Satan win!

As for God, His way is perfect; the word of the LORD is flawless. He is a shield for all who take refuge in Him.

Psalm 18:30

All Scripture is God-breathed and is useful for teaching, rebuking, correcting and training in righteousness.

2 Timothy 3:16

Praise be to the LORD, who has given rest to His people Israel just as He promised. Not one word has failed of all the good promises He gave through His servant Moses.

1 Kings 8:56

When Your words came, I ate them; they were my joy and my heart's delight, for I bear Your name, O LORD God Almighty.

Jeremiah 15:16

I remember Your ancient laws, O LORD, and I find comfort in them.

Psalm 119:52

This is the covenant I will make with the house of Israel after that time, declares the Lord. I will put My laws in their minds and write them on their hearts. I will be their God, and they will be My people.

Hebrews 8:10

"If My people, who are called by My name, will humble themselves and pray and seek My face and turn from their wicked ways, then will I hear from heaven and will forgive their sin and will heal their land."

2 Chronicles 7:14

Come near to God and He will come near to you.

James 4:8

God, to me, it seems, is a verb,
not a noun, proper or improper.
~ *Richard Buckminster Fuller*

❧

Dear Father, You are a verb! Your action in life; loving and forgiving; is what makes peace possible for me. Thank You for being You!

Amen.

Peace in Your Heart, Mind and Soul

Some people are really good at showing peace outwardly. These people don't seem to struggle with the circumstances life deals them. They seem unflappable as they calmly and peacefully accept things ... at least on the surface.

Many times these people confidently proclaim their trust in God. Perhaps they even think they honestly do trust Him. It's easy to fool yourself, especially when you know it is the "Christian" thing to do. The problem is that some of these people may be literally churning with anxiety and worry inside. Sadly, too often this results in actual physical illness.

True peace must run deeper than just the surface. It is not peace if you don't honestly and truly trust God and believe that He is in control of all things. Peace sinks deep into your heart, mind and soul. True peace is complete. Submitting completely to God is the only way to attain this peace. Stop fighting Him, just trust Him and rest in His peace.

You have made known to me the path of life; You will fill me with joy in Your presence, with eternal pleasures at Your right hand.

Psalm 16:11

"When you pass through the waters, I will be with you; and when you pass through the rivers, they will not sweep over you. When you walk through the fire, you will not be burned; the flames will not set you ablaze."

Isaiah 43:2

The LORD is near to all who call on Him, to all who call on Him in truth.

Psalm 145:18

If from there you seek the LORD your God, you will find Him if you look for Him with all your heart and with all your soul.

Deuteronomy 4:29

The LORD is good to those whose hope is in Him, to the one who seeks Him.

Lamentations 3:25

"Ask and it will be given to you; seek and you will find; knock and the door will be opened to you."

Matthew 7:7

Jesus replied: "Love the Lord your God with all your heart and with all your soul and with all your mind."

Matthew 22:37

"For where your treasure is, there your heart will be also."

Luke 12:34

God makes three requests of His children: Do the best you can, where you are, with what you have, now.

~ *African Proverb*

❧

Dear Father, thank You for working in my heart, mind and soul. Thank You for watching out for me through the good times and the bad.

Amen.

Peace in the Midst of Grief

When your heart is breaking, the last thing you want to hear is pious comments about trusting God and His will and submitting completely to Him ... even if you know that all those things are true. Intense grief needs comfort, patience and compassion. Even the basic truths of spiritual trust must be couched in kindness and understanding.

It's not easy to find peace in the midst of grief because some part of the foundation in your life has been shaken. Even if your head knows how trustworthy God is, your heart is screaming in pain. So, what's the answer? Time. Cut yourself some slack and allow yourself time to work through the grief. Maintain your relationship with God. Talk to Him every day and ask Him to heal your pain and guide you to emotional wellness.

One day you will come to realize that God is with you and has been all along. You will feel the comfort and love that only He can give and you will experience peace.

May our Lord Jesus Christ Himself and God our Father, who loved us and by His grace gave us eternal encouragement and good hope, encourage your hearts and strengthen you in every good deed and word.

2 Thessalonians 2:16-17

"Blessed are those who mourn, for they will be comforted."

Matthew 5:4

"I have told you these things, so that in Me you may have peace. In this world you will have trouble. But take heart! I have overcome the world."

John 16:33

Cast all your anxiety on Him because He cares for you.

1 Peter 5:7

He heals the brokenhearted and binds up their wounds.

Psalm 147:3

"For God so loved the world that He gave His one and only Son, that whoever believes in Him shall not perish but have eternal life."

John 3:16

Praise be to the God and Father of our Lord Jesus Christ, the Father of compassion and the God of all comfort.

2 Corinthians 1:3

"So do not fear, for I am with you; do not be dismayed, for I am your God. I will strengthen you and help you; I will uphold you with My righteous right hand."

Isaiah 41:10

God, who foresaw your tribulation, has specially armed you to go through it, not without pain but without stain.

~ C. S. Lewis

❧

Dear Father, thank You for going through painful times with me. Thank You for giving me what I need to persevere. Father, thank You for the possibility of peace in these hard times. I lean on You completely.

Amen.

Being an Example of Peace

Did you know that people are watching you? They are. Those who know that you claim to be God's child watch to see how you handle stress, problems, grief and pain. They watch to see if the way you live matches the words you speak. If the two don't match, you might as well stop talking about trusting God – no one will believe you.

New Christians, younger believers, children, those who are struggling ... all will look to you as an example of someone who lives in peace with God.

Make every effort to be an honest representative of one who has peace. Allow those who watch you to see your struggles and thus understand that peace does not come easily. A commitment to work through problems and trust God, no matter what, brings true peace. Don't make the mistake of faking peace in order to look good. Find true peace and be an example to others. Give God the glory for guiding you to this point.

In everything set them an example by doing what is good.

Titus 2:7

"You are the salt of the earth. But if the salt loses its saltiness, how can it be made salty again? It is no longer good for anything, except to be thrown out and trampled by men."

Matthew 5:13

All of you, clothe yourselves with humility toward one another, because, "God opposes the proud but gives grace to the humble." Humble yourselves, therefore, under God's mighty hand, that He may lift you up in due time.

1 Peter 5:5-6

His delight is in the law of the LORD, and on His law he meditates day and night.

Psalm 1:2

"He must become greater; I must become less."

John 3:30

"Blessed are the pure in heart, for they will see God."

Matthew 5:8

Be strong and courageous. Do not be terrified; do not be discouraged, for the LORD your God will be with you wherever you go.

Joshua 1:9

How great is the love the Father has lavished on us, that we should be called children of God! And that is what we are!

1 John 3:1

Preach the gospel at all times and when necessary use words.
~ *Saint Francis of Assisi*

Dear Father, help me to be an example of Your love and peace to all I come into contact with. Father, guide my thoughts. Help me to trust in You always.

Amen.

Peace When Things Look Dark

Having peace in your life when things are going well is a piece of cake. When your marriage is thriving, your children are happy, your health is good and your career is taking off ... of course you are peaceful. You praise God for His blessings in your life. But what happens when your life slowly falls apart? Where is the peace when your marriage is shaky, or someone you love is sick or you lose your job? Can you find peace then?

Those dark times of life are when peace is most needed. You want to know that God is with you, loving you and helping you. How do you find it? True peace is found only in trusting, honoring and obeying God. The relationship with Him requires a commitment of spending time with Him and keeping your heart quiet enough to hear Him speak.

When things in life get tough, instead of questioning God continually, spend even more time in His Word and be still and listen for His words of comfort and love.

He who ignores discipline despises himself, but whoever heeds correction gains understanding.

Proverbs 15:32

"Be still, and know that I am God; I will be exalted among the nations, I will be exalted in the earth."

Psalm 46:10

After the earthquake came a fire, but the Lord was not in the fire. And after the fire came a gentle whisper.

1 Kings 19:12

In Him our hearts rejoice, for we trust in His holy name.

Psalm 33:21

When I called, You answered me; You made me bold and stouthearted.

Psalm 138:3

And we know that in all things God works for the good of those who love Him, who have been called according to His purpose.

Romans 8:28

He tends His flock like a shepherd: He gathers the lambs in His arms and carries them close to His heart; He gently leads those that have young.

Isaiah 40:11

For just as the sufferings of Christ flow over into our lives, so also through Christ our comfort over-flows.

2 Corinthians 1:5

The ultimate measure of a man is not where he stands in moments of comfort and convenience, but where he stands at times of challenge and controversy.

~ Martin Luther King, Jr.

❧

Dear Father, I need You most when life gets tough. Thank You for Your strength and help. Thank You, Father, for taking control of my life. I know I can trust You always.

Amen.

Reminders of Peace

Perhaps you've heard the story of the wife who is yearning to hear her husband say, "I love you." His response to her is, "I told you once that I love you. If I change my mind, I'll let you know." God isn't like that. His Word tells you over and over that He loves you. He wants good things for you. He has a plan for your life. God knows how your emotions work ... He made them. In His infinite grace, He provides reminders of His love and peace that are available if you just trust in Him. His Word is filled with those reminders.

Your life is filled with peace reminders too: The support base you have of family and friends who love you. The solid teaching available through the multitude of churches in your town. Hundreds of teaching, training and encouraging books in bookstores and libraries.

Notice the sun rising and setting; flowers; animals; trees; oceans; mountains ... God is present. Allow these reminders of God to direct your heart to trust in Him and have peace.

I lie down and sleep; I wake again, because the LORD sustains me.

Psalm 3:5

The LORD gives strength to His people; the LORD blesses His people with peace.

Psalm 29:11

The peace of God, which transcends all understanding, will guard your hearts and your minds in Christ Jesus.

Philippians 4:7

Aim for perfection, listen to my appeal, be of one mind, live in peace. And the God of love and peace will be with you.

2 Corinthians 13:11

Sons are a heritage from the LORD, children a reward from Him.

Psalm 127:3

"By this all men will know that you are My disciples, if you love one another."

John 13:35

Hope does not disappoint us, because God has poured out His love into our hearts by the Holy Spirit, whom He has given us.

Romans 5:5

Neither height nor depth, nor anything else in all creation, will be able to separate us from the love of God that is in Christ Jesus our Lord.

Romans 8:39

I would rather have eyes that cannot see; ears that cannot hear; lips that cannot speak, than a heart that cannot love.

～ *Robert Tizon*

❧

Dear Father, all around me are reminders of how much You love me. Those reminders give me such peace as I think about Your love and care. Thank You for each gentle reminder.

Amen.

Peace in the Midst of Problems

How do you react when the subtle problems of life begin to pile on? They come one at a time – none of them are a big deal individually – but one day you suddenly realize you are weighed down by the sum of them. This weight pushes some women to various ways of attempting to squelch the pain: overeating, alcohol, extra-marital affairs, depression ... yeah, it's not pretty.

You know the answer to how to handle this pain: trust God. Yes, that is the answer. But how do you get there? It takes a day-by-day, moment-by-moment commitment. Begin by giving just one of those problems to God. Really give it to Him. Let Him guide your thoughts so that each time it pops into your mind, you can give it to Him again.

For as long as it takes, work on giving God that one thing. When you've truly let go of that thing, move on to another. As you see God working, guiding and handling your life, you will begin to trust Him more. Peace follows trust.

Trust in the Lord with all your heart and lean not on your own understanding; in all your ways acknowledge Him, and He will make your paths straight.

Proverbs 3:5-6

The way of a fool seems right to him, but a wise man listens to advice.

Proverbs 12:15

I will instruct you and teach you in the way you should go; I will counsel you and watch over you.

Psalm 32:8

You discern my going out and my lying down; You are familiar with all my ways.

Psalm 139:3

If any of you lacks wisdom, he should ask God, who gives generously to all without finding fault, and it will be given to him.

James 1:5

This is the confidence we have in approaching God: that if we ask anything according to His will, He hears us.

1 John 5:14

In their distress they turned to the LORD, the God of Israel, and sought Him, and He was found by them.

2 Chronicles 15:4

Do not be anxious about anything, but in everything, by prayer and petition, with thanksgiving, present your requests to God. And the peace of God, which transcends all understanding, will guard your hearts and your minds in Christ Jesus.

Philippians 4:6-7

Peace is not something you wish for; it's something you make, something you do, something you are, and something you give away.

~ *Robert Fulghum*

❧

Dear Father, I couldn't make it through the difficult times of life if it weren't for You. Your peace is all I need. Thank You for peace. Help me to share it with all I meet.

Amen.

Peace Is a Gift

If you are a mom you no doubt have had the feeling of wishing you could protect your precious children from all the pain and grief of life.

You would like to be able to give your child a world filled with love, acceptance and joy. A good parent protects her child by teaching him or her what's dangerous, what's safe, what's wise and what's foolish. Think about this – God is your parent. He loves you and has similar wishes to protect you from pain and grief. However, some lessons must be learned through the experiences of pain. But your loving heavenly Father does not turn away to let you go through those experiences alone. He walks beside you, in front of you and behind you.

Whatever comes your way in life remember that you are not alone. Let God grow your faith and trust in Him. He loves you and has provided the immeasurably wonderful gift of peace that comes from trusting that He is always with you. Always.

But if from there you seek the Lord your God, you will find Him if you look for Him with all your heart and with all your soul.

Deuteronomy 4:29

Come near to God and He will come near to you.

James 4:8

"Here I am! I stand at the door and knock. If anyone hears My voice and opens the door, I will come in and eat with him, and he with Me."

Revelation 3:20

Examine yourselves to see whether you are in the faith; test yourselves.

2 Corinthians 13:5

This righteousness from God comes through faith in Jesus Christ to all who believe.

Romans 3:22

Therefore, since we have been justified through faith, we have peace with God through our Lord Jesus Christ.

Romans 5:1

He redeemed us in order that the blessing given to Abraham might come to the Gentiles through Christ Jesus, so that by faith we might receive the promise of the Spirit.

Galatians 3:14

In Him and through faith in Him we may approach God with freedom and confidence.

Ephesians 3:12

God proved His love on the Cross. When Christ hung, and bled, and died, it was God saying to the world, "I love you."

~ *Billy Graham*

❧

Dear Father, what an amazing gift Your love is. I'm so thankful for it because it paves the way for peace in my heart – peace that comes only from Your love.

Amen.

Peace in Service

Tennis players know the wonderful feeling of hitting the tennis ball in exactly the center of the racket. It's called the sweet spot of the racket head. You can control the ball best from that spot. It has good spin and is hit with power. Are you wondering what this sweet spot has to do with peace? Read on.

It's easy to get busy serving God. Most churches are happy to let you do all jobs you're willing to take on. You may find yourself doing jobs you aren't qualified for and involved in ministries for which you have no passion. Since that's not much fun, those jobs often feel like work.

The pressure to accomplish tasks for which you are not equipped causes great stress. You'll find joy in service for which you are gifted. Peace accompanies you as you recognize that this job is God's, not yours. Being in the place God has made for you, using the gifts He has given you, doing the job He has for you has been described as being in God's sweet spot.

For great is the LORD and most worthy of praise; He is to be feared above all gods.

Psalm 96:4

Be very careful to keep the commandment and the law that Moses the servant of the LORD gave you: to love the LORD your God, to walk in all His ways, to obey His commands, to hold fast to Him and to serve Him with all your heart and all your soul.

Joshua 22:5

Two are better than one, because they have a good return for their work: If one falls down, his friend can help him up. But pity the man who falls and has no one to help him up!

Ecclesiastes 4:9-10

Learn to do right! Seek justice, encourage the oppressed. Defend the cause of the fatherless, plead the case of the widow.

Isaiah 1:17

"For whoever wants to save his life will lose it, but whoever loses his life for Me will find it."

Matthew 16:25

Whatever you do, work at it with all your heart, as working for the Lord, not for men.

Colossians 3:23

For it is by grace you have been saved, through faith – and this not from yourselves, it is the gift of God – not by works, so that no one can boast.

Ephesians 2:8-9

If anyone has material possessions and sees his brother in need but has no pity on him, how can the love of God be in him?

1 John 3:17

If the world is cold, make it your business to build fires.

~ Horace Traubel

❧

Dear Father, it is such a privilege to be able to serve You – to do Your work on earth. Thank You for trusting me with it and for giving me what I need to do it. Help me to be peaceful in the knowledge that I am serving You in exactly the way You want me to.

Amen.

Peace in Weakness

Have you ever said, "I can't" because the work was too hard or the job was too big? Perhaps you felt that you weren't equipped for what was being asked of you, so the easiest thing to do was simply walk away. It's not that you are afraid of hard work, but some tasks just seem beyond your abilities. Walking away is the easy thing to do, but not always the good thing to do. Walking away means no new experiences and no chance for growth.

However, here's some good news about taking the easy way out ... God is strongest in your weakness. How about that? It's okay to be weak! Recognizing your inabilities and weakness as you understand your need for God's strength and power relieves a great deal of stress. You can do whatever God asks you to do with His strength leading the way. What peace that gives! The pressure is off because all you need to do is to rely on God, trust in Him and follow His guidance and direction.

Be very careful to keep the commandment and the law that Moses the servant of the LORD gave you: to love the LORD your God, to walk in all His ways, to obey His commands, to hold fast to Him and to serve Him with all your heart and all your soul.

Joshua 22:5

Come and see what God has done, how awesome His works in man's behalf! He turned the sea into dry land, they passed through the waters on foot – come, let us rejoice in Him.

Psalm 66:5-6

"Watch and pray so that you will not fall into temptation. The spirit is willing, but the body is weak."

Mark 14:38

There are different kinds of gifts, but the same Spirit. There are different kinds of service, but the same Lord. There are different kinds of working, but the same God works all of them in all men.

1 Corinthians 12:4-6

But He said to me, "My grace is sufficient for you, for My power is made perfect in weakness."

2 Corinthians 12:9

I pray also that the eyes of your heart may be enlightened in order that you may know the hope to which He has called you, the riches of His glorious inheritance in the saints, and His incomparably great power for us who believe. That power is like the working of His mighty strength.

Ephesians 1:18-19

But you, dear friends, build yourselves up in your most holy faith and pray in the Holy Spirit.

Jude 20

I can do everything through Him who gives me strength.

Philippians 4:13

Do not pray for easy lives. Pray to be stronger men. Do not pray for tasks equal to your powers. Pray for powers equal to your tasks.

~ *Phillips Brooks*

Dear Father, I know I can do nothing without You. Your strength is what keeps me going. Thank You for giving me strength to do the work You give me. Thank You for the strength to love others and to serve them. Thank You for the peace that comes from knowing Your strength is guiding me.

Amen.